THE KNEE DESIRES THE DIRT

A Play in Two Acts
by
JULIE HÉBERT

Dramatic Publishing
Woodstock, Illinois • England • Australia • New Zealand

*** **NOTICE** ***

IMPORTANT BILLING AND CREDIT REQUIREMENTS

All producers of the play *must* give credit to the author(s) of the play in all programs distributed in connection with performances of the play and in all instances in which the title of the play appears for purposes of advertising, publicizing or otherwise exploiting the play and/or a production. The name of the author(s) *must* also appear on a separate line, on which no other name appears, immediately following the title, and *must* appear in size of type not less than fifty percent the size of the title type. Biographical information on the author(s), if included in this book, may be used on all programs. *On all programs this notice must appear:*

"Produced by special arrangement with
THE DRAMATIC PUBLISHING COMPANY of Woodstock, Illinois"

At the very center of the problem is the naked cold deadness of one's own self, the only reality in nature of which we can have absolute certainty, and it is unmentionable, unthinkable.

— Lewis Thomas
Lives of a Cell

Women's Project & Productions, Julia Miles, Artistic Director and Patricia Taylor, Managing Director, presented the world premiere of *THE KNEE DESIRES THE DIRT* on October 27, 1998, at Theatre Four in New York City. The production was directed by Susana Tubert and included the following artists:

CAST

Christine .... BARBARA GULAN
Xavier .... AL ESPINOSA
Denise .... SARAH ROSE
Althea .... LYNN COHEN
Jerry................................ REED BIRNEY

Set Design........................ PETER HARRISON
Costume Design .... TRACY DORMAN
Light Design .... DAVID HIGHAM
Original Music/Sound Design .... FABIAN OBISPO
Production Manager .... KEN ALLAIRE
Production Stage Manager .... BRYAN SCOTT CLARK
Casting............................ HARRIET BASS
Press Rep. ...... SPRINGER/CHICOINE PUBLIC RELATIONS

AUTHOR'S NOTE

I encourage the use of a stage curtain, a grand drape, which may be made of burlap, or velvet, or scrim, or rocks, or photographs, or something else. Since Denise addresses the audience directly, she can play outside this boundary.

Part of the time the playing area is a graveyard. Most of the time it is an overgrown backyard garden and part of a tired two-story Victorian house. The setting descriptions within the body of the play are fairly realistic, in an effort to give the right feeling for the environments. However, it seems important that the design not be realistic, as significant parts of the play take place in dreams and other inner worlds.

THE KNEE DESIRES THE DIRT

A Play in Two Acts
For 2 Men and 3 Women

CHARACTERS

ALTHEA PITRE . . . . a woman in her 60s

CHRISTINE PITRE ABRIL . . . . Althea's daughter,
        in her mid-30s, teaches biology at a small college

DENISE ABRIL . . . . Christine's 13-year-old daughter

JERRY LAMBERT . . . . . Christine's boyfriend, in his 30s

XAVIER ABRIL . . . . Christine's dead husband

SETTING: Thibodaux, Louisiana.

TIME: The present.

ACT ONE

SCENE ONE

SETTING: *CHRISTINE's classroom in a small college.*

AT RISE: *CHRISTINE, mid-thirties, wears a wrinkled linen suit. She generally looks intelligent, attractive, preoccupied. She has long hair, tied back. She attempts to walk to a lectern, but is intercepted by XAVIER. XAVIER, late twenties, rugged, wears workman's clothes that have been burned. He looks as if he's been through a fire, charred. CHRISTINE slips into his arms for the briefest moment, then pulls away, trying to get to the lectern. He doesn't release her, she relents. They dance slowly in a dark deeply romantic light. DENISE enters, looks at the lovers, looks at the audience, then settles herself in an area near the edge of the stage. DENISE wears oversized khaki pants, a man's large plaid shirt, and boots. Suddenly, CHRISTINE lurches away from XAVIER, as if waking from a dream. Pulling herself together, finding a textbook at her lectern, she addresses her students [the audience].)*

CHRISTINE. I'm not here. I apologize... On time. *(Looking around.)* I mean. I wasn't again... sorry. At least a few of you hung in and waited. Thank you. Let's, we'll get into Chapter Three today. *(Looking at her watch.)*

We have a little time left. *(She begins lecturing, focused, professional, vital.)* In your mother's womb, you... started... as a single cell. And just as life on earth evolved from single-celled bacteria, to fish to amphibians to mammals, so did you, *in utero.* At one point you had a tail, a single, fish-like kidney and gills. You destroyed these and used the remains to grow legs, two human kidneys and lungs. You went through brain after brain, ending, finally with one, the only one like it, equipped for language. The evolution of a fetus parallels the evolution of mankind. Three-and-a-half billion years of emergence compressed into nine months. Directed by some miraculous cellular memory, you created, destroyed, created and lived through the heaving history of the world, all while your pregnant mother went to the grocery or watched TV. Where is that brilliance today in us, that power... that profound knowledge?

(XAVIER approaches, stands behind her, presses against her.)

Good thing we don't have to do it now, right? Build ourselves from scratch... we'd get it wrong. Misplace the heart, forget to assemble the spine...

(XAVIER strokes her head, her arms, distracting her somewhat.)

Or we might panic at the massive destruction, billions of cells, of You, had to be killed off day after day to make room for change. Death on a scale so vast... by the time you were born, more of you had died than survived.

Your newborn body, strung with flags of memory, jammed with carcasses ...

XAVIER. What a nice carcass you have.
CHRISTINE *(turns into XAVIER's arms, smiling)*. Merci.
XAVIER. *De rien.*

(She slips into an internal reality, walks around him, touching, admiring, loving him. Presumably, in the classroom reality, the students simply see her standing, staring, silent ... lost in thought.)

CHRISTINE. It seems solid, a body ... though made of atoms, made of memory, mostly space ... solid to hold onto, to touch, the curve, the muscle, to smash, bone to bone, pelvis to pelvis, and gaze, eye to eye, in the dark, rods, cones, dim light, adjusting to the ghosts, reflections, the hovering-you in the mirror. I see you best at night in the dark, bone to bone.
XAVIER. I can't keep my hands off you. *(Playful, he grabs her. She darts away, he chases.)* I'm going to steal you. Wrap you in my colors, tattoo you with kisses, mark you, change your name ... *(Catches her.)* And never let you go.

(After a beat, CHRISTINE realizes she's in the middle of a class.)

CHRISTINE *(back to her students, embarrassed)*. Chapter Three. Did I mention that already? A single cell. From one splintering brilliance to many dull worries. Taxes, a better toothpaste, Grade Point Averages ... is that the journey? What have we forgotten? *(The bell rings. Quick, to her departing students:)* Wait. What's the page number? *(Flips through her book.)* Chapter Three, take a look at it.

XAVIER. Let go. You are mine, I am yours, *c'est tout.*

CHRISTINE. The ground recedes. My flags carry me away. The dream is terrible and I love the dream.

(Lights rise on DENISE, who addresses the audience.)

DENISE. I don't know why people don't talk about sex. Walking around all day nice as pie, "How you doing?" "What grade are you in?", as if they don't go sticking fingers and tongues and penises and breasts all over the goddamn place at night. People everywhere do it all the time and never admit it. Like even the ultra-religious. It pisses me off. It's misleading. Like, where do you find out the real deal? I know about condoms and date rape and STD's, but, like where do I find out about, you know, how to do it right? Not the movies, not that romantic, crappy-happy-ending stuff. *(She makes a face dismissing all TV and film romances.)* Like, you know, can it be like, honest? I don't want to wear lipstick, or... *(She pushes her breasts up as if in a WonderBra.)* "Oh, my darling...you're so h-h-h-h-o-t-t-t-t."...you know? *Seven Steps to Good Sex for Teens.* Where's that documentary? *(DENISE leads the way into the next scene.)*

SCENE TWO

SETTING: *CHRISTINE's old house is a two-story, unpainted Victorian. The backyard is wildly overgrown. There is a four-foot brick wall, faded reddish-brown under peeling whitewash. Weeds have taken hold in some of the cracks.*

AT RISE: *Later that afternoon. DENISE hops up, sits on the wall, watches. ALTHEA hacks her way through the weeds. She wears a coordinated shorts set, matching turban and tennis shoes. She has a scarf tied around her neck. Tiny and intense, she whacks grasses and vines that have been thickening for years. She barely dents the dense underbrush. CHRISTINE enters the scene, sees her mother, rushes over.*

CHRISTINE. Stop. What are you doing?

ALTHEA. How can you stand these weeds?

CHRISTINE. I like it overgrown. Leave it.

ALTHEA. I will not. It's a fire hazard. Not to mention allergies, snakebite... God knows what all is up in here.

CHRISTINE. I like it.

ALTHEA *(stopping)*. These are weeds.

CHRISTINE. One woman's weed's another woman's garden.

ALTHEA. Crap. I know a garden when I see one and this isn't it. But, we WILL have a working garden by next spring... pole beans, squash, okra, cabbage. Tomatoes and cucumbers over here. Big rectangle outlined in Brown-eyed Susans. Rows of sunflowers in the back. And I think Confederate jasmine up against the house.

It'll climb the wall so people might not notice the lack of a paint job.

CHRISTINE. Mom, I like my house unpainted, my plants growing wild. It's a choice.

ALTHEA. You don't have to worry about the work, I know you're busy. I'll do it. I'm living here now and I do the work of two men, you know I do. *(Standoff. Two stubborn gals.)* How about we make a deal...you don't paint the house and I'll take care of the yard.

CHRISTINE. You miss your garden. Is that it?

ALTHEA. You're home early.

CHRISTINE. Not really.

ALTHEA *(checking her watch)*. You're not due back till...

CHRISTINE. Oh shit. My faculty meeting. *(She starts to leave.)*

DENISE. It's too late, Mom. By the time you get back there, it'll be over.

(CHRISTINE stops, embarrassed.)

ALTHEA. Knucklehead. How the hell I raised such a *couillon* [fool], I'll never know.

DENISE. They say some traits, like common sense, skip a generation.

CHRISTINE *(snapping into control)*. You shouldn't be doing all this anyway. How're you feeling?

ALTHEA *(impenetrable)*. Fine, and you?

CHRISTINE. What did the doctor say? You had an appointment today, right?

ALTHEA. Same old double-talk. Weather channel says sun's coming out. When's your "lover" getting here?

CHRISTINE. Don't call Jerry that.

ALTHEA. That's what you call him.

CHRISTINE. Just call him Jerry.

ALTHEA. He's got your car?

CHRISTINE. He'll be back at four.

ALTHEA. He'll be late.

CHRISTINE. Did the doctor say whether the tumor has gotten smaller?

ALTHEA. Those damn doctors. First of all, you can't understand what the hell they're saying. Second of all, even if you could understand it, they're not going to tell you what they really think. And third, even if they told you what they actually thought, it doesn't mean jackshit. They don't understand why people die. How people die. How people live. Did you know that George Washington had a head cold and a slew of doctors bled him to death ... to cure him of something that would have gone away by itself in seven days. Did you know that?

CHRISTINE. Where'd you get that?

ALTHEA. Read it. Fifty years from now they're going to laugh about the treatment I'm getting, radiation and chemotherapy. They're poisoning me. They might as well just slit the veins and let the blood run out. If the disease doesn't get you, the cure will. I'm so sick of doctors.

CHRISTINE. They're doing the best they can.

ALTHEA. Yeah, well, they can bite me.

CHRISTINE. Not in front of Denise.

ALTHEA. I picked it up from her.

CHRISTINE. So I have to call the doctor to find out what he told you?

ALTHEA. I didn't go.

CHRISTINE. What?

ALTHEA. I didn't go. I threw the pills away. I'm finished with all that.

CHRISTINE. With all what? Medicine? Are you crazy?

ALTHEA *(outraged)*. Look at this.

CHRISTINE. Mom, you can't do this.

(ALTHEA pulls the scarf away and unbuttons some of her shirt, revealing marks on her neck and chest, lines, circles, angles in blue, red, brown and green.)

ALTHEA. Did you know some of this is permanent?

CHRISTINE. I was with you when they did it.

ALTHEA. I've had enough degradation.

CHRISTINE. Ma ...

ALTHEA *(covering herself)*. There are a few things I want to do, and I want to do them in peace. I'm sorry I'm a burden on you. I'm sorry I don't drive. I'm sorry I'm living in your house, but I can't stop any of that any-more. Just because you're helping me, doesn't mean you can tell me what to do. I haven't been a child for a long time. *(Exits.)*

DENISE. She's right.

CHRISTINE. Don't you get tired of taking whatever posi-tion is opposite to mine?

DENISE. No. She can do what she wants. She can die how she wants.

CHRISTINE. We're all on our own, is that it? Flailing in the breeze ... ?

(Lights up on XAVIER. CHRISTINE switches into an in-ternal reality, naming the trees, talking to XAVIER. DENISE simply sees her mother silent, staring, spaced.)

CHRISTINE. *Melia azedarach.* Chinaberry. *Albizia juli-brissin.* Mimosa. What's that tree? So green against the rain clouds ...

DENISE. Mom ...

CHRISTINE. Oh, I know the name of that thing ...

DENISE. Mom.

CHRISTINE *(without looking at DENISE).* What? *(To XAVIER.)* I'm always surprised at the sound of my voice. There's an apology in the very tone of my voice. I'm lost in some debate in my head, working it out ... and then someone serves me a cup of coffee or whatever, and I hear a voice, "Oh. Thank you very much." Whose voice is it? Sweet, delicate, apologetic. Certainly not the voice that's just been thinking ... This girl's voice, this child's voice is an embarrassment.

(DENISE starts to walk away. Lights out on XAVIER.)

CHRISTINE. Denise. Come with us.

DENISE. No, thanks.

CHRISTINE. It's All Saints' Day.

DENISE. So?

CHRISTINE. Come on. We'll whitewash Grandpa's gravestone, we'll sit by the water, it'll be nice ...

DENISE. I've got homework. *(They look at each other, a million miles apart.)*

CHRISTINE. We could stop for ice cream ...

DENISE. Or maybe you could buy me a Barbie doll.

CHRISTINE *(defeated).* Okay. *(Walks off.)*

DENISE *(to the audience).* Right. And then, the other thing, is like, who cares? We live on a planet orbiting one of a hundred billion stars, on the edge of one of a

hundred million galaxies. Obviously, nothing we do matters. Nothing will be remembered. Nothing makes a difference. People are like insects chewing up the planet,
doing whatever fucked-up-ed-ness they can dream up. I
mean, why think twice about anything? Just go for it. I
don't know.

*(JERRY enters the garden in a hurry. He's dressed in a
suit, not too expensive, not too cheap. He wears a polo
shirt underneath it. His loafers are worn.)*

JERRY. Hey, Denise, where's your mother? We're supposed to be going now.

DENISE. Althea said you'd be late.

JERRY. I'm not late. It's four-fifteen.

DENISE *(shrugs, existential)*. Nothing really matters, does
it?

JERRY. You're telling me. *(He starts to exit.)*

DENISE. Hey, Jerry, what's the secret to life?

JERRY *(pointing to her like the swinger that he is)*. Louis
Prima. *(He exits.)*

DENISE. Good answer. *(To the audience.)* Who's Louis
Prima?

(Lights up on CHRISTINE, alone. JERRY finds her.)

JERRY *(imitating Louis Prima)*. Hey, hey. Gotta go, gotta
go.

CHRISTINE. You're late and then you rush us?

JERRY *(singing, sort of)*. "Baby, just one look at you, my
heart goes...teeep-sy in me."

CHRISTINE. I'll get my mother.

JERRY. How long's this going to take?

(CHRISTINE silently assesses the situation for a moment.)

CHRISTINE. You know. I think it's not such a good idea. Your coming with us.

JERRY. I said I'd do it, I'll do it. No big deal.

CHRISTINE. I don't want to rush her.

JERRY. No rush. How long does it take to whitewash a headstone? I've got to be back on the road by six. Plenty of time.

CHRISTINE. That might not work. Maybe you should find another way...

JERRY. Oh. Fine. At the last minute, cut me off. Leave me hanging.

CHRISTINE. I'm just trying to... I don't want... I can't really deal with the pressure so well today.

JERRY. What pressure? It's four o'clock now...

CHRISTINE. It's almost four-thirty.

JERRY. We have plenty of time.

CHRISTINE. I'll get her.

JERRY. Give me a kiss.

(She does. It's easier than refusing. He looks at his watch and exits. CHRISTINE wakes ALTHEA.)

CHRISTINE. Mom. He's here. We can go now.

ALTHEA *(sits up, looking frail and old)*. I'm forgetting something.

CHRISTINE. What?

ALTHEA. I don't know. It's just that feeling.

CHRISTINE. I know that feeling. *(They descend the stairs.)*

DENISE *(writing).* Althea, what's the first thing you remember? Ever. In your whole life.

CHRISTINE. Why?

DENISE. I have to write a paper.

CHRISTINE. Well, what's the first thing you remember?

DENISE *(matter-of-fact).* Sitting on my dad's lap and he seemed really big.

CHRISTINE. You recall that?

DENISE. That's about all I remember of him.

CHRISTINE. You must have been two or three...

DENISE. Althea?

ALTHEA. Oh, Lord, I don't know. Something about a cat.

DENISE. What about the cat?

ALTHEA. I can't remember that far back.

DENISE *(gives ALTHEA a microcassette recorder).* Here, take this tape recorder and tell me cool stuff about when you were little. Like what was the first TV show you remember?

ALTHEA. There was no TV.

DENISE. Whoa. What did you do?

ALTHEA *(trying to remember).* I don't know. We played. In the yard. In the grass. In the mud. *(Beat.)* Why do you dress like this? Like an old man.

DENISE. Why do you wear a turban? *(Reaching for ALTHEA's head.)* Take it off. It'd be totally rad.

ALTHEA *(holding her turban protectively).* Enjoy your beauty, while it lasts.

(She kisses DENISE then exits. CHRISTINE double-checks her purse.

DENISE. Mom, can I sleep at Catherine's house tonight?
CHRISTINE. I thought you had homework.
DENISE. We'll do it together.
CHRISTINE. Did her mother say it was all right?
DENISE. Yes.
CHRISTINE. Okay.
DENISE. Okay.
CHRISTINE. How will you get over there? Jerry's taking my car.
DENISE. Her mother'll pick me up.
CHRISTINE. All right.

(JERRY re-enters briefly.)

JERRY. Christine. Let's go.
CHRISTINE *(to DENISE)*. See you tomorrow, then.

(CHRISTINE exits. During the following speech DENISE uses a piece of chalk to draw out a hopscotch map on the stage floor. She addresses the audience.)

DENISE. There's this girl I know, at school ... and there's this guy in her class, who's kind of a badass ... not really bad, but he smokes and ... he's got, like, a motorcycle. He's one year older than the other kids in the class, 'cause he failed, but they gave him an IQ test and he blew them away. That really pissed them off, that he was so smart, but he failed anyway. And this girl kind of likes him. He's really cute. In fact, they're kind of like going together, kind of. And he touched her. You know, down there. And ... you know this girl is really cool, so she didn't want to freak-out like a child or anything, so she didn't say anything. But. It was weird. And so now, this guy ... wants the girl to tell her mom she's sleeping at a friend's house and go on an all-night motorcycle ride with him. And she kind of wants to. And she kind of doesn't. *(DENISE hopscotches from one to heaven, with heavy stomping jumps, then stops, catches her breath and walks offstage without looking at the audience.)*

SCENE THREE

SETTING: *Graveyard. There is a desecrated grave, topped by a small, once-whitewashed stone with a barely readable name, JOSEPH PITRE. The gravesite is overgrown, unkempt, littered with remains from a party.*

AT RISE: *As ALTHEA and CHRISTINE come upon Joe's trashed-out grave, we hear a tugboat horn from the industrial canal nearby. This place is not idyllic. ALTHEA carries a covered bucket filled with whitewash, a paintbrush and a purse. CHRISTINE has a small lawn chair.*

ALTHEA. Oh my God.
CHRISTINE. It's all right, Mom.
ALTHEA. Oh my God.

(CHRISTINE looks around, steps in mud.)

ALTHEA. Look at this.
CHRISTINE. I see it.

ALTHEA. It's...it's too far for me to come every week, damn it. Damn it.

CHRISTINE. It's not your fault.

ALTHEA. Oh my God.

CHRISTINE. Sit down. Here. *(She unfolds the chair. AL-THEA sits in it.)*

ALTHEA. He'll never forgive me.

CHRISTINE. Oh, Ma, Papa doesn't care.

ALTHEA. How do you know?

CHRISTINE. Don't worry. It was just kids having a party.

ALTHEA. Why don't they go next door, to Mr. Lucky's club? Right there. There's a bar right there.

CHRISTINE. Probably under-age. Got their beer and came over here.

ALTHEA. Goddamn it. *(She stands.)* No respect for the dead. No respect for the dead.

CHRISTINE. Take it easy.

ALTHEA. I'm not taking it easy. That's what the spies said in World War II...the traitors, the collaborationists... those Vichy's...Mata Hari, "Take it easy." I'm not taking it easy...in the face of insult...in the face of... *(She attacks the litter, melted candles, etc., on the grave.)* Look at this. *(She hurls empty beer cans and wine bottles.)* Look at this. *(She sees something else.)* Oh, God. Sweet Jesus, save us all. *(She gets gardening gloves from her purse.)*

CHRISTINE. What?

(ALTHEA reaches onto the grave and with horror, pulls up a used condom.)

ALTHEA. Disgusting. Look what he's been through.

CHRISTINE. Good grief, Mom. It's just a condom.

(With morbid interest, ALTHEA holds the condom at arm's length.)

ALTHEA. Why do people come to graveyards to drink and have sex? I don't get it. When I'm in the ground I hope someone tries to have sex on my grave, I'll scare the shit out of him. He'll never have sex again.

CHRISTINE. At least he used a condom.

ALTHEA *(looks at her as if she's a cockroach)*. What are you, looking on the bright side?

(CHRISTINE finds a used plastic supermarket bag and offers it as a trash bag.)

CHRISTINE. Here.

ALTHEA *(presenting the condom)*. Look at it. A little snapshot of the poor pitiful world.

CHRISTINE. Get rid of it.

ALTHEA *(drops the condom into the bag)*. We should have brought garbage bags.

CHRISTINE. Who knew?

(Together they begin to pick up litter. ALTHEA holds up a cigarette butt.)

ALTHEA. There are cigarette burns on your father's grave. Burned. *(She holds the cigarette butt up as proof of man's inhumanity to man.)* Cigarette burns.

CHRISTINE. Papa was a smoker...

ALTHEA. What?

CHRISTINE. What?

ALTHEA. What.?

CHRISTINE. What? It just occurred to me ...

ALTHEA (gives her a look and flicks the butt far away). I swear. You want your weaknesses burned onto your headstone?

CHRISTINE. I won't care.

ALTHEA (mocking). "I won't care." Every direction you turn, every minute of the day ... the decay of civilization. By the time Denise dies, there won't be graveyards. Take up too much room. They'll recycle all her parts ... they'll be recycling skin and bones by that time ... then incinerate the remaining debris like so much chicken fat. There goes Denise, sssssszzzzzz. (Almost talking to herself.) People. I swear. I used to be able to tolerate them, now I just can't stand them. My ambition is to get through the rest of my life encountering as few people as possible.

CHRISTINE. That shouldn't be too hard, the way you act.

ALTHEA. Soon we'll have to go to the moon to find tranquility.

CHRISTINE. I know a place called Solitude Road ...

ALTHEA. What?

CHRISTINE. An old road in the woods by a pig farm. Fat sows dozing under ancient oaks ... (They stare at each other for a beat.)

ALTHEA. What are you talking about?

CHRISTINE. What? Tranquility ... you said ...

ALTHEA (shaking her head in disgust). I'm talking about dignity, and privacy, for the dead ... not laziness ... Speaking of, where's Jerry?

CHRISTINE. He went to Mr. Lucky's for a minute.

ALTHEA. Drinking in the afternoon. That's a good sign.

CHRISTINE. He's got a big meeting tonight, he's a little nervous.

ALTHEA. Oh, good. Drinking'll help.

CHRISTINE. Just relax.

ALTHEA. What's the matter with him?

CHRISTINE. Nothing.

ALTHEA. He doesn't act like a man.

CHRISTINE. What are you talking about?

ALTHEA. What's Jerry good for?

CHRISTINE. You tell me.

ALTHEA. Nothing.

CHRISTINE. He drove us out here.

ALTHEA. You can drive. It's your car.

CHRISTINE. He wanted to come. It was a gesture.

ALTHEA. Such a gesture, he had to immediately disappear to have a drink.

CHRISTINE. He'll be back.

ALTHEA. So? Then what? He'll watch us work. Probably give us tips.

CHRISTINE. See. He acts like a man.

ALTHEA *(repeatedly snaps her fingers in CHRISTINE's face).* You're wasting your time. You're wasting your time with him.

CHRISTINE. Ma ... stop it. *(CHRISTINE pulls away from the snapping.)*

ALTHEA. He's a joker like all the rest of them you've ... been with.

CHRISTINE. No. Not ...

ALTHEA. What then? What is it about this guy? Sex? You're joking me, right?

CHRISTINE. He's kind.

ALTHEA. Kind?

CHRISTINE. He makes me laugh. He doesn't...

ALTHEA. ...require much attention? *(Resumes cleaning.)* When was the last time you went to Xavier's grave?

(XAVIER appears.)

CHRISTINE. I don't go there.

ALTHEA. You should take Denise.

CHRISTINE. I don't like to go there.

ALTHEA. Why not?

(CHRISTINE shakes her head, says nothing. XAVIER stands apart from her.)

ALTHEA. He was your husband. You've got to keep up his grave.

CHRISTINE *(looking to XAVIER)*. He's not there.

ALTHEA. If you don't do it, who will? It's probably a worse mess over there than it is here.

CHRISTINE. It's a mausoleum.

ALTHEA *(attacks the trash vigorously, disgusted)*. Help me. Can I get some help here? *(ALTHEA works, cleaning and pulling weeds. CHRISTINE talks, ALTHEA doesn't hear her.)*

CHRISTINE. The Prisoner's Dilemma. Cooperate or Resist. In all dilemmas of survival...the question is, "Do I cooperate with my opponent or confront?" Who triumphs most often, do you think...the warrior or the peacemaker?

(XAVIER hands CHRISTINE her textbook and glasses. She walks to her lectern, addressing her class.)

CHRISTINE. Do nice guys finish last? Or do nice guys last longest? A computer experiment was set up, a series of tournaments...experts from all over the world submitted strategies...complex approaches, simple approaches; devious plans, random attacks, nice-guy, let's-all-work-together tactics... All pitted against each other, and themselves, each battle run two hundred times, the entire tournament repeated five times.

There was a hands-down, clear-cut winning strategy. What do you think it is? Before I tell you, I want you to write an essay arguing your point of view, using biological examples. What insures survival? Cooperation or Aggression?

XAVIER *(hands her an envelope)*. You've been fired.
CHRISTINE. What? *(She opens the envelope, reads the paper inside.)*
XAVIER. You've been fired.
CHRISTINE. They can't do this, I love teaching, I need teaching.
XAVIER. They say you refused to use the proper textbook.
CHRISTINE. It's outdated. Their book is boring.
XAVIER. They say you've missed many classes.
CHRISTINE. I have.
XAVIER. They say you're chronically late.
CHRISTINE. I am. I step out of time with you, I lose the clock... I'm sorry, I won't...

XAVIER. They say the students are confused and unprepared for future classes.

CHRISTINE. No. I love teaching, I'm a good teacher. Opening their minds, making cross-connections, stimulating their curiosity with my own. That's me, isn't it? Isn't that me anymore?

XAVIER. They say they've replaced you as of next week.

CHRISTINE. Mid-semester? *(Suddenly.)* My students... *(She hurries back to her lectern, to explain, to apologize...)*

XAVIER. They're gone.

(XAVIER walks away. From where she is, CHRISTINE addresses ALTHEA, who continues to work at the grave.)

CHRISTINE. I'm thinking about taking a trip.

ALTHEA. What kind of trip?

CHRISTINE. I don't know. *(Lying.)* Maybe a sabbatical.

ALTHEA. You don't have tenure, for God's sake.

CHRISTINE. I need a break.

ALTHEA. You only work nine months a year as it is.

CHRISTINE. Mom. Be on my side for five seconds.

ALTHEA. I'm always on your side. Somebody's got to bring your head in from the clouds.

CHRISTINE. Thank you. Thank you so much.

ALTHEA. Don't use that tone with me.

CHRISTINE. Could we not fight? Is that possible?

ALTHEA. I'm not going to pretend your half-baked ideas are okay. Not me.

CHRISTINE. I need to get out of here for a while.

ALTHEA. This is not a good time.

CHRISTINE. Why? Because you stopped taking your medicine and anything could happen? I'm supposed to be on red alert for the next ... until ...

(They both stop, arrested by the thought of ALTHEA's death.)

ALTHEA. I'm sorry.

CHRISTINE. No. I'm sorry. I'm sorry.

ALTHEA. I should never have sold my house.

CHRISTINE. This is not about that.

ALTHEA. I should have known better.

CHRISTINE. No. I ... I ... I got ...

ALTHEA. What?

CHRISTINE. I got, you know ...

ALTHEA. No, I don't know.

CHRISTINE *(lying)*. A warning.

XAVIER *(as he goes offstage)*. Coward.

(CHRISTINE gives him a look.)

ALTHEA. A warning for what?

CHRISTINE. Being late. Missing class.

ALTHEA. You're the teacher.

CHRISTINE. I drift away, like time is not the same for me. Time flies ... but it also drips, gets stuck, moves slowly, sideways, backwards ... time is just a concept we all agree on, isn't it?

ALTHEA. No.

CHRISTINE. ... like moving the clock forward in the spring, back in fall, doesn't that strike you as the strangest thing? Why don't we all agree to skip Tuesdays in

April and have extra Wednesdays in May? Time is whatever we say it is.

ALTHEA. If that was so, nobody'd get old.

CHRISTINE. Maybe that's why it feels good to slow it to a
crawl.

ALTHEA. Like a sow under an oak.

CHRISTINE. I think you should take your medication.

ALTHEA *(stops)*. That's for me to decide.

CHRISTINE. I can't ignore your mistakes either.

ALTHEA. I know what I'm doing.

CHRISTINE. What would Papa say? He'd make you take
the chemo.

ALTHEA. I don't know about that. *(Sound of fiddle music.)*
I don't know what he'd say.

CHRISTINE. You miss him?

ALTHEA. Not really. We just weren't suited for each
other, Christine. I can't stand fiddle music. Can you
imagine that? Live with somebody for thirty-seven years
and you're not suited to them. People used to do that all
the time. Not anymore. I guess that's a sign of progress.

CHRISTINE. I was suited to him. He'd wait up for me and
we'd sit and talk with some crazy Japanese movie on.
Bad dubbing. Monster crushing Tokyo. Papa said he
knew my problems were as big to me as his were to
him. We advised each other. It was part of my date, go
out with some goofy boy, come home and talk to Papa
about the important stuff. I felt so respected.

ALTHEA. I never got much of that side of him.

CHRISTINE. You were always busy.

ALTHEA. Too bad daydreaming's not a paying profession,
your father would have been a wealthy man.

CHRISTINE. Mom...

ALTHEA. Don't bother me about the medicine. My mind's made up.

CHRISTINE. Why are you giving up?

ALTHEA. Please, please, please. Let me alone for one minute. Damn it.

CHRISTINE. Sorry.

ALTHEA. I just want a little bit of peace here.

CHRISTINE. Okay. I'll go find Jerry.

(CHRISTINE exits. ALTHEA kneels on the grave, rubs away dirt.)

ALTHEA *(quiet)*. I never asked you for much, but can you help me now? Can you help me for once? *(She tightens her fists and keeps them that way.)* Goddamn it to hell, I can't see what to do. It's coming at me and I can't see. How am I supposed to fix it if I can't see it. I take care of every damn thing in the world that comes my way, I face it square on and handle it. I've been shamed, broken, tired, mocked by my family... I've been the man and the woman... all my married life... *(She touches the gravestone.)* ...you know it. And I don't care, I did it, I just keep going... a tiny mule pulling the weight of my whole damn family. I can take it. But this is making me mad. What do I do if I don't know what to do?

(XAVIER appears in the background. ALTHEA doesn't see or hear him.)

XAVIER. Leave room for grace, *ma vieille*. [Old woman.].

ALTHEA. I want to fix. I want to do. I have so much will-power... *(Clenches fists.)* I have things to take care of, I

can't... I hate doctors, I hate priests, I hate my body...
(She grabs at her chest.) Get this thing out of me. Are
you there? *(She makes tight fists, straining to hear, hear
anything. She listens, nothing.)* No one helps. No one
ever helps. No one ever gives me anything. If I need it, I
have to take it. Push, grab, push out of the way. Grab it.

XAVIER. Don't grab. Idiots, children and criminals grab.
Fais pas ca. [Don't do it.]

(She doesn't hear him.)

ALTHEA *(cynical snort, referring to the graveyard, the silence).* This is a big joke. So what? I'm used to being
alone. *(She pulls weeds from around the edges of his
stone.)* It doesn't matter, there's nothing to do. I don't
want help. I'll deal with it when it comes. By myself,
like always. *(Overcome, eyes closed, she rocks back and
forth, weeds and dirt in her fists.)* Leave me. Leave me.
Leave me. *(She puts both her palms flat on her neck.)*
Leave me. Leave me.

*(Lights crossfade to JERRY who stands at the bar in Mr.
Lucky's club, having a bourbon. CHRISTINE sits next to
him, nursing a beer. She's in a deep funk, he doesn't
notice at first.)*

JERRY. I was voted most likely to succeed in my senior
class in high school. Did you know that? Did I ever tell
you that? Damn straight, Goddamn it. They knew it. My
friends. They knew.

CHRISTINE *(wants him to keep talking).* What?

JERRY. That I was gonna make it.

CHRISTINE. Umm.

JERRY. I skipped the ten-year reunion but I will be there at twenty. With bells on. This is the deal, tonight's the night, and Ronnie Kyle is my man. *(Tender.)* I'm going to take care of you. You're going to be a lady of leisure. You can give up teaching.

CHRISTINE *(upset)*. I don't want to stop teaching.

JERRY. Okay. Good. That's good. *(She sips his drink, he pulls her close to kiss her, she resists.)* What's the matter?

CHRISTINE *(pulling away)*. Nothing.

JERRY. Baby, I know you. Something's been bugging you all day. *(No answer.)* You can tell me. It's just me. *(She waves it all away.)* Come on. What is it? I have bad breath?

CHRISTINE *(laughing)*. No.

JERRY. You hate my haircut?

CHRISTINE. I love your haircut.

JERRY. What do you know? Did something right. *(He presses her.)* What is it?

CHRISTINE. My mother stopped taking her chemo.

JERRY. When?

CHRISTINE. I don't know when. She skipped an appointment with her oncologist yesterday.

JERRY. What are you going to do?

CHRISTINE. What can I do? Force her?

JERRY. Did you talk to her?

CHRISTINE. She won't talk to me. You know how she is.

JERRY. Hey. She's going to take a break till the pain starts. Then she'll get scared and start up again.

CHRISTINE. Maybe. It'll be too late.

JERRY. Baby. *(He watches her for a second, deciding whether to speak.)* It's already too late.

CHRISTINE. You don't know that.

JERRY. Okay.

CHRISTINE. Nobody knows that.

JERRY. Okay. Okay. *(They look away from each other.)* Look, we'll talk to the doctor next week, okay? I'll go with you, we'll talk to him, see what's really up. All right?

CHRISTINE. All right.

JERRY. She's just scared.

CHRISTINE. Me, too.

JERRY. Hey, hey now. *(He puts his arm around her, kisses her. She is not comforted, but tries not to let him see that.)* No blues today, okay? *(He sings, Louis Prima style, snapping his fingers, softly swinging.)* "Cause I'm the Sheik-y man...that's who I be." *(She smiles at him.)* That's my girl. No blues, okay? Not today, know what I mean. *(She nods, she knows the pressure he's under.)* Do I look like a winner to you?

CHRISTINE. Definitely.

(Lights up on ALTHEA who kneels on Joe's grave, head down, palms flat, rocking a little. JERRY and CHRISTINE approach. He's concerned about getting mud on his clothes.)

CHRISTINE. Mom?

ALTHEA *(turns, surprised to see them)*. Where've you been?

CHRISTINE. Nowhere.

ALTHEA *(getting up, getting busy)*. There's work to do.

JERRY. What work?

ALTHEA. Clean up around here. Do this right. Do it proper. Cut the grass.

JERRY. We didn't bring a lawn mower.

ALTHEA. Whose fault is that? That's the man's job.

CHRISTINE. Mom, we're just going to whitewash and put out the flowers.

JERRY. Anyway, it's time to go.

ALTHEA. I'm not finished.

JERRY. You should have brought some garbage bags.

ALTHEA. Is that a tip? *(They stare at each other.)*

JERRY. Five minutes. We've got five minutes.

ALTHEA *(stares at him without moving, intimidating him)*. Who's got five minutes?

JERRY. We've got to leave in five minutes.

ALTHEA. Why?

JERRY. I, uh...I... *(Caught in ALTHEA's cobra-like gaze, he can't speak.)*

CHRISTINE. Jerry's got a meeting with a backer for his new business.

ALTHEA. I came here for a reason.

CHRISTINE. We'll help you. Come on. *(Takes the whitewash, starts to paint the grave.)* We can whitewash in five minutes.

(ALTHEA doesn't move. She addresses JERRY, who also doesn't move.)

ALTHEA. Who are you? To rush me? *(Uncomfortable, JERRY averts his eyes.)* A man with a plan?

(Lights fade as CHRISTINE quickly whitewashes her father's headstone. She chatters nervously.)

CHRISTINE. What is the name of that tree? I've been trying to think of it all morning. *Nigra, nigra*...something, something *nigra. Quercus* is oak. Crape myrtle is *liquidambar styraciflua*... *Nigra* ssss—something nigra. It's a willow. Good God, I'm supposed to know this.

(XAVIER appears. As lights fade on this scene, CHRISTINE walks toward him and the next scene begins.)

SCENE FOUR

AT RISE: *Later that night in the backyard. CHRISTINE walks to XAVIER as she speaks.*

CHRISTINE *(quiet)*. You held me on your lap that first night, sitting on a straight-backed chair, looking out the open door on the cane fields. There was a moon. There was rain, tapping on the tin roof through the night. Our eyes adjusted to the dark and we sat all night, watching the mist, the sky, the sugar cane, the woods...and never looked at each other to break the spell. *(He takes a handful of her hair and pulls her head back, gently yanking it over and over like reins.)* I have not touched, never touched, anything like you, like me, so long ago. It marks me. The impossibility of that touch. *(He releases her hair, she turns to him.)* Why are you back now? *(He doesn't answer.)* I gave myself to you without looking that night.

XAVIER. Give yourself again.

CHRISTINE. What do you mean?

XAVIER. Give me a part of you.

CHRISTINE. What part?

XAVIER. Eyes, heart, neck, hair.

CHRISTINE. Foot. *(Laughing, holding it up.)* You can have my left foot.

(He drops down near her ankle. The movement in this sequence is stylized, no attempt is made at realism. She reports numbly as if in a car wreck.)

CHRISTINE. He becomes savage, bites my ankle. The bone snaps. I hear it crunch. I look and my foot is gone, the bone sticks out from the flesh. What do I do now? His mouth is bloody but he is civilized again as he pulls my foot from his mouth. I feel like maybe I've made a mistake. I have crippled myself. *(She turns to XAVIER, who is wiping his mouth.)* Have I made a mistake?

XAVIER *(stands, holding her shoe)*. You need me now.

CHRISTINE. Can't you give me my foot back?

XAVIER *(walks away, carrying the shoe)*. You gave it away.

CHRISTINE. How do I walk? Was this a mistake? Why do you want my foot?

XAVIER. Questions asked too late.

(ALTHEA enters wearing a long, starched nightgown, sipping an elegant glass of creme de menthe. CHRISTINE looks at her, coming back to reality.)

ALTHEA. What you're calling kindness in Jerry is not kindness. It's indifference. *(CHRISTINE doesn't answer.)* In a few years, Denise will be gone to college, gone. And I will be gone. What will become of you? You going to sit still while Jerry, or someone just like him, borrows your car, borrows your money, borrows your body? *(CHRISTINE gets up to walk away.)* You don't seem to mind people borrowing your life in general. You're not using it.

CHRISTINE *(softly)*. Stop it.

ALTHEA. Don't you have dreams?

CHRISTINE. I drowned in my dream last night. An inch beneath the surface.

ALTHEA. You know what I mean. Don't you want anything?

CHRISTINE. All of a sudden you're interested, as a mother ... cancer gives you insight ... to see the screw-ups, the possibilities, the losses, the amazing losses ... it's too late.

ALTHEA. No, it's not.

CHRISTINE. Mom, I've been here for thirty-seven years and you've barely noticed me, why start now?

(The phone rings. The two women look at each other ... they both know why now. Finally, CHRISTINE leaves to answer the ringing. ALTHEA walks alone in the backyard. The wind is blowing and wheezing slightly.)

ALTHEA. Cold front's coming in. *(She holds her hand up, feeling the wind.)* Are you there? Are you nothing? Are you the wind? Is it too late? *(She listens.)* Silence, nothing but silence. Drifts of things realized and forgotten. Small things. Like luck to be walking here still.

(She pulls DENISE's tape recorder from her pocket and speaks into it.)

ALTHEA. I crawled under the house. It was up on pilings, back in those days. This was below Houma, so it flooded all the time. I was maybe two or three years old. It was one of those white-hot days to blind you. I crawled under there to that shade and, boy oh boy, that black dirt was cool on my skin. I nestled in for a nap ... but next thing you know I hear this hissssss ... I'm eye to eye with a very angry black cat. I remember looking at this yellow eye, one eye, he only had one eye, and some pointed teeth, and hair standing up on his back. I had never seen that, hair standing up like that. I was so curious, staring at that yellow eye, but not scared. Not at all.

Then a kid went by on a bicycle with a playing card clothespinned to the spokes. "Pac-pac-pac-pac-pac" and that cat popped his head around toward it, then together ... we listened ... as it faded off. Slowly, he turned his one eye back on me, his hair flattened and his mouth closed around those sharp teeth. Then suddenly, he dug his paw and flung dirt backward through the air. I was impressed, child. I stared at his backside as he strutted away, holding his tail straight up. He was something. I could have gotten scratched to hell, but I didn't know that, and so I wasn't scared and that's what saved me.

(She turns the tape recorder off. CHRISTINE walks out.)

CHRISTINE. Cold front's coming in.

ALTHEA. I like it when the weather's changing.

CHRISTINE. Too chilly.

ALTHEA. It's going to look good back here when I'm done with it.

CHRISTINE. Wrong time of year for planting.

ALTHEA. Who was on the phone?

CHRISTINE. Jerry, the car broke down. He needed my AAA number.

ALTHEA. Does he need you to wipe his butt, too?

CHRISTINE. Good grief, Mom.

ALTHEA. I'm just saying.

CHRISTINE. Why are you picking on me and Jerry all of a sudden?

ALTHEA. No reason.

CHRISTINE. You want me to be somebody I'm not.

ALTHEA. I don't want you to give up on yourself.

CHRISTINE. You're setting quite an example.

ALTHEA. I'm not giving up. I like to do things my own way, and that's what I'm doing. *(She finds her creme de menthe.)* You, though. We've got to straighten you out.

CHRISTINE. I like Jerry.

ALTHEA. What sort of business is he trying to get into?

(CHRISTINE walks around the backyard, avoiding the subject.)

CHRISTINE. It's a kind of delivery business.

ALTHEA. What's he going to deliver?

CHRISTINE. I don't know.

ALTHEA. WHAT?

CHRISTINE. Snack foods, liquor and videos. He'll make late-night deliveries anywhere in the parish.

ALTHEA *(snickering)*. Bringing junk food to couch potatoes. An idea whose time has come.

CHRISTINE *(snickering with ALTHEA)*. He wants to call it "Don't Get Up."

ALTHEA. He should know. How's he going to deliver all over the parish? *(CHRISTINE shrugs.)* Not in your car.

CHRISTINE. If this backer works out, he can probably buy his car back.

ALTHEA. You need a partner, Christine, not another child to take care of. You need to learn how to say, "No."

CHRISTINE. You need to learn how to say, "Yes."

ALTHEA. To what? I've got no decent offers.

CHRISTINE. Mom...I've got to talk to you...

ALTHEA. No medicine.

CHRISTINE. Not about that.

ALTHEA. What then?

CHRISTINE. My job.

ALTHEA. Get a watch with an alarm that rings five minutes before every class. Good heavens, girl, all you have to do is show up.

CHRISTINE *(giving up, standing)*. You want something to eat?

ALTHEA. Nothing tastes good anymore. They killed off all my taste buds. *(CHRISTINE nods, starts to exit.)* What's wrong with your foot?

CHRISTINE. Nothing.

ALTHEA. You're limping.

CHRISTINE. No, I'm not.

(She exits, not limping. Lights rise on DENISE, sitting on the edge of the stage, a little disheveled, but okay.)

DENISE. It didn't hurt. I didn't feel much and that surprised me. It was like I was numb but my brain was hyperalert. The whole time he was on me I stared at my boots, in the corner of the tent. I've worn these boots so long, they've taken the shape of my feet even though they're hard. I kept thinking how the imprint of my foot would always be on those boots.

Just pushing. No thought. No words. Just do it. He's a nice guy. It didn't take long. And afterward, I was just me, the same old me, and that surprised me. There was no blood. He had a peaceful smile on his face and gentle as anything he said, "You okay?" What could I say? Okay, not okay, whatever.

(ALTHEA stands in the darkest part of the yard, near the brick wall. JERRY dances in, drunk, jingling CHRISTINE's car keys. When she hears him, CHRISTINE comes out, with XAVIER.)

JERRY. I made it, I made it home. Good for me, good for AAA. He had that door unlocked in a flash. Hey, baby. Guess what? I did it. I fucking did it. The old bastard gave me a check. *(He gets the check out of his pocket.)* A check. "Don't Get Up" is a reality. "Don't Get Up." "Don't Get Up."

(ALTHEA watches like a ghost. JERRY kisses his check and tangos. Lights dim on all but CHRISTINE.)

CHRISTINE. Can you be happy in an unhappy world? It seems some people sail above it all, smooth, joyful, lucky. Nobody knows anybody like that close up. Close up we see the scars, the wavering. Close up we are so mortal. So we smile politely, turning from the shocking reminders in other people's faces. Even so. Even though it's a fucking pit we live in and we run around with grinning face masks over our moldy corpses, even so, it seems possible to have a tiny corner of happiness. *(She walks downstage.)* It seems so exquisite at first you don't believe your luck, and you grab at it. Not so fast. All that did was hook you. Like a fishhook piercing your hand, you're invested. If you leave now all you have is your wound. And your lesson. But if you stay, if you stay...what? Are you stupid? Obviously you were baited and hooked. It was a sham, a trick, clearly you're being taunted and you should get away. Blood running down your arm, hand throbbing, you see the bait again, that tiny pocket of happiness that first caught your attention, and you wonder. It still looks good. Well, now that I'm here, now that I've already suffered, I might as well... and you reach with the other hand and whap. Hooked. Both hands sliced and hooked.

Through your tears, blurry, you still can't take your eyes off the bait. The pain, the humiliation, galvanizes you. You will have that happiness. No matter what. Whap. Whap. Both thighs pierced by giant fish hooks. Suspended in agony, you cannot see anything else. Nothing else is real to you except your pain and the singular vision of your own happiness. If I had less of a dream, maybe the price wouldn't be so high. Bargain hunting in the fucking pit. *(She turns to look back at XAVIER.)* Of course, it too, the bait, the dream, looks different close up ... not quite as exquisite. And I am now not the shockingly beautiful young Narcissus that first leapt at this vision. *(She walks back to him, climbs into his lap.)* But anyway, I'm here, I've paid, and if I concentrate, I can block out the compromises ...

(ALTHEA turns, hand to her chest.)

CHRISTINE. And the moans.

(DENISE touches her own face.)

DENISE. I want to look at my face in a mirror to see if I can tell the difference. *(DENISE exits hurriedly.)*

END OF ACT ONE

ACT TWO

SCENE ONE

AT RISE: *It is three weeks later, the Wednesday evening before Thanksgiving. The weather has changed and it is much colder. CHRISTINE sits next to a thawing turkey and chops vegetables. XAVIER sits in an improbable place. He wears her high-heeled red shoe on one foot.*

CHRISTINE *(as if lecturing to her class).* There's a mass in the middle of your brain, discovered over forty years ago and still today no one knows what it's for. The Medial Forebrain Bundle, what a terrible name...it's nickname is...

(XAVIER waits.)

...The Pleasure Center. It receives and sends silent PLEASURE, continuously, autonomously. Below the level of consciousness. How does it work? Why is it there? No one knows. It has nothing to do with the senses, or sex, or hunger, or beauty or anything like that. What is this news constantly streaming through the nervous systems of all animals? It must signify something essential, something necessary for life. *(Aside to XAVIER.)* I miss giving lectures.

XAVIER. Give it to me.

CHRISTINE *(giving him the lecture)*. Some say the impulses coming in from cells all over the body, bear the news...they are alive. Simple as that. It seems essential to life that you are aware you are alive. A subtle sensation, easily missed in the roar of the self. Pleasure in being alive.

XAVIER. We have that. Together.

CHRISTINE. I don't think it's something you can have together. I think it's a function of the individual. Maybe knowing you are alive, means knowing you are alone.

XAVIER. You are not alone, never will be. *(She looks at him...wondering...just the tiniest crack in her faith. He sees it.)* I need another part of you. *(He approaches her.)*

CHRISTINE. I'm having trouble walking now.

XAVIER. This will make you stronger. *(He delicately embraces her. As always, she can't resist him.)*

CHRISTINE. Nothing makes sense anymore. Footsteps tap, tap, tap in the hall, conversations make shapes in the air. You, chasing me through the woods, falling, kissing my thigh, I feel that...carried weightless by your muscles, my blood pumped by your huge heart... *(He strokes her hair. She pulls away from him.)* I know this is wrong, all wrong.

XAVIER. Give me your hair.

CHRISTINE *(holding onto her hair)*. No. I can't. I can't give you anything more.

XAVIER *(gentle, docile)*. Give yourself to me. *(He waits, still. She shakes her head no.)* I take care of you.

CHRISTINE. I've lost my job...

XAVIER. It doesn't matter.

CHRISTINE. I can't keep pretending to go to work. Soon I'll run out of money. Soon they'll find out. What then?

XAVIER. Come to me.

(He opens his arms slightly, inviting her in. She considers, silently, wanting to go to him, knowing it's wrong. Finally, she takes a step toward him when DENISE enters.)

DENISE. What are you doing?

CHRISTINE *(recovering)*. Chopping. Chopping. Chopping vegetables for the stuffing. For tomorrow. For Thanksgiving. Does Catherine want to come over for Thanksgiving?

(XAVIER retreats, watches the scene.)

DENISE. I don't know.

CHRISTINE. You can invite her, okay?

DENISE. Okay. Can I ask you a question?

CHRISTINE. Sure.

DENISE. What happened when you first had sex?

CHRISTINE. Oh, that question.

DENISE. You don't have to tell me, if you don't want to.

CHRISTINE. You're not thinking of having sex?

DENISE. No.

CHRISTINE. You're too young to have sex.

DENISE. I know, Mom. Give me a little credit. I'm just curious.

CHRISTINE. I had a boyfriend with the patience of a glacier.

DENISE. How old were you?

CHRISTINE. Seventeen. *(DENISE nods.)* Inch by inch he crept, over two and a half years. And then, when it finally happened...yuck. I didn't like him, I didn't like myself, I didn't like how it felt, I didn't like where we were. It was a disaster.

DENISE. So what'd you do?

CHRISTINE. I broke up with him and pretended it never happened. About a year later, I fell in love with your dad.

DENISE. Xavier. It's such a cool name.

CHRISTINE. He was a cool guy.

DENISE. Did you tell him?

CHRISTINE. About the other guy?

DENISE. Yeah.

CHRISTINE. Eventually.

DENISE. What'd he do?

CHRISTINE. Laughed. He didn't care about that. He always made me feel like, I don't know, I was all right, he was all right, we were just people and things were fine.

DENISE. I feel so tricked I didn't get to know him.

CHRISTINE. Me, too. You have a great dad.

DENISE. I don't have a dad.

CHRISTINE. Hey, now.

DENISE. What was it like when you first did it with Xavier?

CHRISTINE. That's, that's kind of private.

DENISE. Oh.

CHRISTINE. I mean, I, we, knew it was special.

DENISE. How'd you know? You don't have to tell me, like, the details, or anything, but, I mean...how'd you know?

CHRISTINE. I felt like I'd known him forever. And when we finally, were going to, you know, go for it ... it was like, like my body knew what to do.

DENISE. What does that mean?

CHRISTINE. My body responded in grown-up ways and it shocked me really, but there was no mistaking this was different than the other guy, this was the right thing to be doing. We were in love ... and it felt great.

DENISE. You must've been so sad when he died. I mean, who ever heard of a ship burning in the middle of the ocean.

CHRISTINE. They didn't know he was sleeping down there.

DENISE. What happened?

CHRISTINE. You know.

DENISE. I know the little-kid version ... tell me again.

CHRISTINE. He was working offshore to make money which he could do faster in the gulf than he could as a history teacher.

DENISE. How'd the fire start?

CHRISTINE. A gas pipe exploded. A small boat was docking next to the rig, and it hit this pipe ... which broke. The natural gas ignited from the boat's engine ... and the fire raced through the pipe, exploding all over the rig. Everybody got off okay, except your dad. He was sleeping below deck. I don't think he woke up. He just went deeper into his dreams, deeper inside. I don't think he suffered.

DENISE. I don't think so either.

CHRISTINE. No. Anyway.

DENISE. Did you ever, I don't know, like, feel his presence or anything like that?

CHRISTINE *(laughs a little)*. At the funeral I had you and I couldn't make it to the mausoleum. So a few days later I went there and even though I had directions for exactly where he was buried, I couldn't find him. I went round and round this marble maze with dead people stacked to the ceiling, more frantic by the second. The guard said it was time to lock up, I had to leave in two minutes. Weeping, running around with my tea roses, I tore around a corner and slammed into a stone angel. Instantly, I knew. I started laughing. It was Xavier, telling me how silly I was, how it didn't matter where his body was, because he wasn't there anymore. He was with me, wherever I was. I plopped the roses into the nearest vase and that was that. Did I ever tell you that?

DENISE. No.

CHRISTINE. I see his eyes in your face.

DENISE. Cool. Maybe I'll have his point of view. *(Gets up to leave.)* I'm going over to Catherine's.

(DENISE ducks out. XAVIER crosses to where she was.)

CHRISTINE. Again?

DENISE. See you.

CHRISTINE. Invite her to come over for Thanksgiving tomorrow.

DENISE *(offstage)*. Okay.

CHRISTINE *(to XAVIER)*. When she was little, I could feel her in my belly across a room, my body reeling her in as she ran to me. She was mine like my arm is mine. She doesn't need me anymore.

XAVIER. I need you. *(He rakes her hair.)* And you need me.

(She leans into him, letting her head go. ALTHEA walks in from the backyard, carrying empty plastic flats which previously held small green plants. She looks thinner, weaker. CHRISTINE slowly sits up straight. XAVIER exits.)

ALTHEA. I didn't know you were back.

CHRISTINE. Mom, this is a terrible time to plant.

ALTHEA *(puts the flats down)*. Look, there's something I have to tell you.

CHRISTINE. Just sit at the table with us tomorrow. Okay? You don't have to eat.

ALTHEA. A woman called here for Jerry. *(Silence for a moment.)*

CHRISTINE. Yeah? So? He's not here.

ALTHEA. She said he was supposed to pick her up at the airport, but her flight's running late. The girl at the office thought she might reach him here.

CHRISTINE *(covering, cool)*. Did you tell her he's not here.

ALTHEA. Yeah.

CHRISTINE. I'll give him the message when I see him.

ALTHEA. I thought you should know.

CHRISTINE. Thanks. Did she leave a number?

ALTHEA. No. *(Grabs a bottle of Miracle-gro.)*

CHRISTINE. All those stupid plants are going to die before Christmas.

ALTHEA. Maybe. *(Starts to leave, then stops herself.)* You going to do something? *(CHRISTINE stops, looks at ALTHEA.)* You going to ask him about this? *(No answer.)* Because if you don't, I will.

CHRISTINE. Don't you dare.

ALTHEA. Somebody has to. If I know you, you're going to let him get away with this. You're going to let him lie.

CHRISTINE. This is none of your business.

ALTHEA. You're my daughter.

CHRISTINE. So what?

ALTHEA. Standing still is the wrong move.

CHRISTINE *(starts to leave)*. I don't give a shit what Jerry does.

ALTHEA. You little coward. Even dying, I've got more spunk than you.

CHRISTINE *(stops)*. I know you can't stand me.

ALTHEA. That's not true.

CHRISTINE. Because I stole Papa from you.

ALTHEA *(taken aback)*. What?

CHRISTINE. You're jealous.

ALTHEA *(after a silence; quietly)*. It's a bad deal. With Jerry.

CHRISTINE. We talked about you, Papa and me. All the time. You were our problem and we discussed how to handle you.

ALTHEA. Handle me? *(They look at each other for a beat.)*

CHRISTINE. "Get out of my way." "Get out of my sight."

ALTHEA. I can't remember.

CHRISTINE. What's to remember? You never had the time. For anything. For me, for him. No one would come to the house. You were mad all the time.

ALTHEA. I had reason to be.

CHRISTINE. Everybody was in your way. Slowing you down.

ALTHEA. If I didn't do things, they didn't get done.

CHRISTINE. We were strangers, Mom. Still are. *(She goes inside.)*

ALTHEA. "I don't have time." What was I in such a hurry to do? *(There is a silence as she remembers.)*

(JERRY enters, in a hurry. ALTHEA pulls herself together.)

JERRY. Where's Christine?

ALTHEA. Why don't you leave Christine alone?

JERRY. I don't hurt Christine.

ALTHEA. You sure?

JERRY. Not as much as you do.

ALTHEA. Hah. You're out of your territory, boy. You don't know what you're talking about. She's my flesh.

JERRY. That doesn't mean anything.

ALTHEA. To you.

JERRY. What does it mean, Althea? Tell me what it means.

ALTHEA *(thinks for a moment)*. It means I can never get rid of her. And she can't get rid of me. No matter what.

JERRY *(ironic)*. You think that's a good thing?

ALTHEA. Keeps you honest. You don't have that with her, Jerry. It makes you lonely. Prone to lying.

JERRY. I'm going to find Christine.

ALTHEA. She's waiting for you. *(JERRY bounds upstairs. ALTHEA digs violently in the dirt.)* Damn it to hell, have I been alive? I can't remember? *(She digs, then ...)*

XAVIER. You gonna grab death, too? *(She slows her digging.)* Ton genou desire la terre. [Your knee desires the dirt.] *(Almost a prayer.)* La terre se rappelle de toi.

ALTHEA. *La terre se rappelle de toi.* The dirt remembers me. *(She holds the dirt in her hands, feeling it, smelling it. Remembering, very private.)* Bare knees in damp dirt digging. Dirt. A childhood spent in dirt. And mud. Rich Louisiana loam. Grass stains on my feet, mud under my toenails, earthworms wiggling. Dirt on my face. A world of dirt and mud and loam. A child swimming in the earth.

(Lights dim on ALTHEA and come up on JERRY as he slides into CHRISTINE's room, in a good mood.)

JERRY. Hey, babe. How're you doing?

CHRISTINE. Fine.

JERRY. I need to borrow the car an hour early tonight.

CHRISTINE. Need to pick someone up at the airport? *(Silence between them.)*

JERRY. Yeah. How'd you know?

CHRISTINE. She called here. Looking for you. So I called her back.

JERRY. Did you reach her?

CHRISTINE. Will my answer determine the extent of your lie?

JERRY. Fuck you. Come off it. It's nothing. If you reached her, you know that.

CHRISTINE. What's her name?

JERRY. Amy.

CHRISTINE. Who is she?

JERRY. She's an old friend who needed a favor. I said I'd give her a ride from the airport. That's it.

CHRISTINE. In my car.

JERRY. What other car do I have? *(CHRISTINE makes a disgusted sound.)* It's no big deal. You're blowing it out of proportion.

CHRISTINE. Don't lie to me.

JERRY. Whoa. I'm not lying to you. I love you.

CHRISTINE. Don't say that.

JERRY. What? That I love you? What?

CHRISTINE *(pause, as she considers whether to go into a full blown confrontation)*. Nothing.

JERRY. Hey, come on. This is silly. *(She stares at him in silence. He goes over and kisses her.)*

CHRISTINE. What kind of friend?

JERRY. Somebody I knew in college. Coming in to visit her family. *(CHRISTINE shakes her head, it doesn't sound right, but she can't find words.)* Hey, let's not fight. Okay? *(He pulls CHRISTINE's face up by the chin.)* Okay? Be a sport, okay. It's a holiday, business is out the roof, I got to go. I'll be back in the morning and we'll do something special. Hey, tomorrow's Thanksgiving, I'll take you out.

CHRISTINE. I'm cooking.

JERRY. Am I invited? *(She doesn't move.)* Hey. Who loves you? *(She hands him the car keys. He takes them.)* Who loves you?

CHRISTINE. You do.

JERRY. Okay. All right? Don't fret about this, okay? It's nothing. I'll call you from work in the middle of the night and tell you I love you, okay? *(CHRISTINE nods.)* Okay. Can I come over for Thanksgiving tomorrow?

CHRISTINE. Yeah.

JERRY. Okay, I'll see you then. I'll bring the wine. *(He kisses her again. Suddenly, she grabs onto him, kissing him passionately. He breaks away.)* Hey now.

CHRISTINE. What?

JERRY. We don't have time for that ...

CHRISTINE. Come on. *(She brings his hand to her body. He pulls away.)*

JERRY. I'm sorry, baby. Can I have a rain check? *(She says nothing.)* I'll see you tomorrow, you steamy thing. Be sweet. *(He leaves. She looks out the window.)*

CHRISTINE. *Salix nigra.* How could I forget that? Black willow. Not a weeping willow, a black willow. *Salix.* Willow. *Salix nigra.*

(DENISE walks up the stairs. She's edgy.)

DENISE. Mom?

CHRISTINE. You're back early.

DENISE. Yeah. What's wrong with Althea?

CHRISTINE. What?

DENISE. She's in the backyard, I don't know, digging ...

CHRISTINE. She's fine, leave her alone. I want you to help me with the cooking tomorrow.

DENISE. Okay.

CHRISTINE *(notices DENISE's shirt)*. Denise. Your shirt's on inside out.

DENISE *(looks, caught red-handed, maybe)*. Oh, wow. I must have worn it like this all day.

CHRISTINE. You did not. It was not like that when you left.

DENISE. It must have been, Mom.

CHRISTINE. Don't lie to me.

DENISE. I'm not lying to you.

CHRISTINE. I said, DON'T LIE TO ME. Don't insult me by lying to me. Why is everyone lying? *(DENISE is silent.)* What does this mean? *(No answer. CHRISTINE hits the wall with her hand. DENISE jumps.)* What does this mean?

DENISE. Nothing.

CHRISTINE. What's his name?

DENISE. What?

CHRISTINE. What's his name?

DENISE. I don't know what you're talking about.

(ALTHEA walks in and watches from the bottom of the stairs, unnoticed.)

CHRISTINE. Have you ... ? Have you ... ? Have you just ... ?

DENISE. I don't want to talk about this.

CHRISTINE. I bet you don't, but we're going to.

DENISE. No, we're not. *(She tries to get up the stairs, past CHRISTINE.)*

CHRISTINE. Yes, we are. *(Grabs her arm, DENISE yanks it away.)*

DENISE. Don't you dare.

CHRISTINE *(grabs her again)*. I dare. I'm your mother.

DENISE *(doesn't resist)*. Face it, Mom. You don't really care. *(She pushes past CHRISTINE into her room. CHRISTINE is stunned.)*

ALTHEA. You're going to let her get away with that?

CHRISTINE *(numb)*. I don't know.

ALTHEA *(mocking)*. "I don't know." You better know. You better go in there with the belt. Tan her hide. Punish her. Find out who this boy is. Talk to his parents. Put a stop to this. Put a stop to this right now. *(CHRISTINE is speechless, trying to think.)* What is wrong with you? *(ALTHEA grabs her by the chin and shakes her.)* Snap out of it. Damn it. Do something.

CHRISTINE *(pushes ALTHEA's hands away).* Stop it.

(ALTHEA loses her balance. CHRISTINE tries to catch her, help her get up. ALTHEA refuses any help.)

ALTHEA. I'll go in there. I'll take care of this.

CHRISTINE *(blocks her way).* No. She is my child.

ALTHEA. You're incapable of ...

CHRISTINE. No. I will handle it. In my way. You stay away from this. I am not incapable.

ALTHEA. You better handle it. You better handle it. She's my granddaughter, and I'm not going to have her flail around like you, if I have anything to say about it. She's not going to go whoring around from man to man. She's not going to start like this. She has to be controlled.

CHRISTINE. Leave her alone.

ALTHEA. You better handle this.

CHRISTINE. I AM NOT A WHORE. You can't call me a whore. Not in my own house. Not anywhere.

ALTHEA *(looks at CHRISTINE, surprised, a little impressed).* I didn't call you a whore.

CHRISTINE. You said, "whoring around."

ALTHEA. Well, what do you call it?

CHRISTINE. I call it having relationships.

ALTHEA. I'll say. Save your daughter.

(ALTHEA goes into her own room. CHRISTINE knocks on DENISE's door.)

DENISE. Stay out.

CHRISTINE. I need to talk to you. *(No answer.)* I won't yell.

DENISE. I don't want to talk to you.

CHRISTINE. Why do you think I don't care? *(No answer.)* Denise?

DENISE. Leave me alone, Mom.

SCENE TWO

AT RISE: *Four a.m. Thanksgiving morning. This scene has three locations. ALTHEA, CHRISTINE and DENISE are in their beds. ALTHEA and CHRISTINE are dreaming, DENISE sleeps fitfully. CHRISTINE sits up in her bed.*

CHRISTINE. The girl is gray, from head to toe, wrapped in gray, sad, her skin is gray, and she needs her warnings.

ALTHEA *(softly)*. Help.

CHRISTINE. I burned her warnings ... she needs her mother to sign them ...

ALTHEA. Help.

(CHRISTINE jumps up in a panic. Her foot gives way and she crashes to the floor.)

CHRISTINE. Where are my shoes? My feet? Running through the ship on fire. Do you have my shoes?

ALTHEA *(looks around as if many people surrounded her)*. A black cat with one yellow eye claws my face, draws blood.

CHRISTINE. My foot? My foot. We are on fire and no one cares.

ALTHEA. I grab her, she bares her teeth, slashing with her back claws. I grab her legs ... *(ALTHEA stops, frozen as if she holds a wild cat.)*

CHRISTINE. I should not be on this great ship without my shoes. I am so mad at him for sending me out barefoot. What was he thinking?

ALTHEA. I can't let her go, I can't move. I try to speak, no sound comes out. She watches me, curled lips, slitted eye. *(ALTHEA throws the cat with great force.)* I throw her from me with all my might.

(XAVIER appears to CHRISTINE.)

CHRISTINE. You push me to fly, but my feet are burnt. He comes in the door, big as a mountain, louder than a jet ...

XAVIER. WHO HAS SET MY SHIP ON FIRE?

CHRISTINE *(whispered echo).* "Who has set my ship on fire?"

ALTHEA. The cat leaps back onto my face and rips my flesh. *(Quiet.)* No.

CHRISTINE. I reach out to him with my flaming arm. He steps toward me with big feet, big shoes. I know he wants to crush me. I scream ...

ALTHEA. "NO."

CHRISTINE. "NO." And run toward him. Toward him. Why toward him?

ALTHEA. Now I watch the cat tear my white skin to shreds.

CHRISTINE. He whispers in my ear... "I take care of you."

XAVIER. I take care of you.

ALTHEA. Me, the woman, the face, the skin, falls to the floor in strips like a cheap Halloween costume.

CHRISTINE. The gray girl wanders the burned-out ship, lost, alone, she calls and calls, with no words she calls out.

ALTHEA. In the waxy mess of my old skin, stands another woman, large, naked, blue, with no expression.

CHRISTINE. Pity floods my heart, I reach for her, she falls into my arms, merging, melting into my body, and I freeze...

ALTHEA. A light glows from her blue body. Her face. I recognize her face.

CHRISTINE *(panicking)*. This girl's not sad, she's DEAD. She jumped into my body so she could die. She wants me to die for her. *(CHRISTINE starts to run, to escape, XAVIER grabs her, startling her, restraining her.)* Don't touch me when I'm naked. Don't touch me in the dark. Don't touch my velvet. *(She tries to shake him off. He strokes her hair, frightening her. She tries to shake him off several times. He strokes harder and harder.)* I'm in the wrong place. I'm the wrong size. I don't belong here anymore. I'm too big, too big for this... what am I doing down here?

(CHRISTINE hears a sound in the hallway. She gets up and finds DENISE, carrying sheets. ALTHEA also begins to move about in her room, awake, searching for something.)

CHRISTINE. What's the matter?

DENISE. I wet my bed.

CHRISTINE. You what?

DENISE. I wet my bed.

CHRISTINE. Good Lord, Denise. You're thirteen years old.

DENISE *(humiliated, ashamed; defensive).* I'm sorry.

CHRISTINE. Oh, honey. I'm sorry. I'm sorry. It's all right, all right? *(CHRISTINE hugs her.)*

DENISE. I'm freaking out, Mom.

CHRISTINE. I know. I know.

(They sink to the floor with the sheets. ALTHEA applies blue eye makeup to her face, neck, upper chest, arms. Her radiation tattoos show through the makeup. She has no turban and is bald.)

CHRISTINE. Did you use a condom?

DENISE. Yeah.

CHRISTINE. Were you ... did you ... I mean, did you agree, did you want this?

DENISE. Yeah.

CHRISTINE. Are you okay? *(DENISE nods.)*

DENISE. I want to go to sleep for a thousand years.

CHRISTINE. That's about how long you're going to be punished.

DENISE. I figured.

CHRISTINE. Who is he?

DENISE. Chris Arnaud.

CHRISTINE. I don't know him.

DENISE. No.

CHRISTINE. Is he older than you? *(DENISE nods. CHRISTINE, ready to kill the older guy).* Oh my God.

DENISE. Almost a year older.

CHRISTINE. Oh. I see. I'm going to have to talk to his mother.

DENISE. I'm sorry, Mom.

CHRISTINE. This was not the first time? *(DENISE shakes her head.)* What is the matter with you?

DENISE. Nothing. Don't yell at me. *(DENISE drops her head, ashamed. CHRISTINE puts her arms around her.)*

CHRISTINE. How many times? *(The phone rings.)* It's Jerry. I'll be right back. *(She gets up and answers it in her room.)* Hello? Yeah. *(Her eyes wander around the room toward the hallway and DENISE. Into the phone.)* I love you, too. Okay. Okay. All right. Okay. *(She hangs up, returns to DENISE.)* How many times?

DENISE. Three.

CHRISTINE. With the same boy? *(DENISE nods.)* No more. You can't do this.

DENISE. How old do you want me to be?

CHRISTINE. Why don't you try to understand the many levels of kissing first?

DENISE. I don't know what the rules are.

CHRISTINE. You know better than this. *(She speaks very quickly.)* Number one. You have to be grown up enough to realize you're not grown up enough for this. Let your body finish growing, for God's sake. Wait until you can vote. Wait until you can drive a car. Wait until you don't have to hide. What's the rush? There's an enormous amount of sex in your future. It's a very confusing thing. Why throw yourself off balance before you even have a grip on who you are, on what you want. *(She takes a breath.)* Number two. It's best if you're in love with the person. Are you in love with Chris Arnaud?

DENISE. No, I don't think so. I mean, he's cool and all, but how would I know?

CHRISTINE. You would know.

DENISE. How?

(The lights go out on blue ALTHEA. CHRISTINE tries to answer honestly, precisely.)

CHRISTINE. You care more about the other person than you do about yourself. It's ... very rare.

DENISE. You want me to wait till I'm married.

CHRISTINE. No. That would be dumb. I certainly wouldn't marry anybody before I had sex with them and I don't expect you to either. But I wish for you that you only have sex with people you love. It's no good to have sex with people unless you're in love. It's a mess.

DENISE. Like with Jerry.

CHRISTINE. Oh, stop. That's complicated, that's different.

DENISE. Are you in love with Jerry? *(Silence.)* For me, things are black and white, for you things get to be gray.

CHRISTINE. You're lucky to have someone make it black and white.

DENISE. It's not though, Mom.

CHRISTINE. You're not old enough for this. Do you think you are? Do you think you're ready?

DENISE. No. But I was curious.

CHRISTINE. Why did you ask me about this tonight, if you'd already done it?

DENISE. I kind of thought there must be more to it.

CHRISTINE. There is more to it. It's deep. But give your-self a chance. There's an unlimited amount of half-assed experiences in the world, but for great experiences, for wonderful times, you have to pay more attention. You have to have the courage to say "no" to the always-available half-assed experience. *(Mocks herself.)* How would I know?

DENISE. Sounds like you do.

CHRISTINE. Why did you say I didn't care about you?

DENISE. Mm-mm.

CHRISTINE. Don't you realize how much I love you?

DENISE. It's like I get it in my head, but sometimes, it's like, you're not there. Like I have to tiptoe around and be careful not to upset you with my real life. *(CHRISTINE takes this in, accepting the blow.)* I'm sorry, Mom.

CHRISTINE. It's okay. Tell me.

DENISE. That's it. It's just that sometimes I feel like if I'm not careful, you're going to break. And sometimes, I just want to, I don't know ... not be so careful.

CHRISTINE. Yeah. I'm sorry. I, I'm not sure why that is. Maybe, I ...

DENISE. What?

CHRISTINE. I miss Xavier. It's like I died when he died, which is a hell of a sorry thing to say to you. *(She holds DENISE.)* Oh honey, I'm sorry. Jesus ...

DENISE. It's okay, Mom.

CHRISTINE. It's not okay. I'm like a ghost wandering through my life and your life, hanging out with men who like women to be ghosts. Good grief. *(She straightens herself up, sighs.)*

DENISE. Mom?

CHRISTINE. Sometimes years seem like minutes. Like a dream told in minutes. *(Standing.)* Let's get some clean sheets.

SCENE THREE

AT RISE: *Thanksgiving morning. ALTHEA has dug up the entire backyard. Upturned dirt is everywhere. She is on her knees digging troughs, digging holes, digging. She is still in her nightgown, still blue, although some attempt has been made to rub it off.*

ALTHEA. No one looks at me. I am secret. I have seen many things. *(She digs in despair.)* I've seen the mud under the house. The plumbing. The angry black cat. I've seen the planks above me shake with heavy footsteps. I've seen the eye, the watery yellow eye... *(She stops digging for a moment.)* What's behind, what's ahead?

(Still in her nightgown, CHRISTINE comes down and sees her mother in the yard.)

CHRISTINE. Mom?
ALTHEA *(startled, opens her eyes, not wanting to be disturbed).* What?

(CHRISTINE walks over, gingerly, afraid to disturb her obviously fragile mother.)

CHRISTINE. What are you doing?

ALTHEA *(starts digging)*. What do you want?

CHRISTINE. Are you all right?

ALTHEA. Yes.

CHRISTINE. What's on your face?

ALTHEA. Eye shadow. I'll buy you some more.

CHRISTINE. You don't need to do that. Why ... why ...

ALTHEA. Because I felt like it. That's all. I wanted to see
what I'd look like if I was blue. This stuff doesn't come
off as easy as it goes on. *(A pause while ALTHEA digs,
CHRISTINE considers.)*

CHRISTINE *(gently)*. What are you doing?

ALTHEA. I haven't lost my mind, you little twerp. Don't
talk to me like I need a strait jacket.

CHRISTINE. Mom, you've got to stop this.

ALTHEA. I can't.

CHRISTINE. What are you doing?

ALTHEA. I'm digging, I'm digging.

CHRISTINE. It's the wrong time of year for planting.

ALTHEA. I'm not planting, I'm digging. I like it, it feels
good.

CHRISTINE. What are you looking for?

ALTHEA. I don't know. I don't know.

CHRISTINE. You have to come in, it's getting too cold. A
front's coming in.

ALTHEA *(stops digging, annoyed at being interrupted)*.
Where's my house? Where's my privacy? Where's my
place to do whatever the hell I want to, even if it doesn't
make sense to anyone else? Where is it? Where is it?
(She's digging again.) I can't find it, I can't find it. I
want to go home and I have no home.

(CHRISTINE goes to ALTHEA, puts her arms around her, tries to stop her.)

CHRISTINE. It's all right, Ma. It's all right.

ALTHEA. NO. It's not all right. *(She breaks free of CHRISTINE's arms. She kneels, quietly, alone.)* What's falling apart here is a lifetime, a lifetime of saying "It'll be all right." Of making things all right. I don't know how to make this all right. And neither do you. *(They look at each other for a moment.)* Did you talk to Denise?

CHRISTINE. Yes.

ALTHEA. Is she punished?

CHRISTINE. Yes.

ALTHEA. Are you going to call the boy's parents?

CHRISTINE. Yes.

ALTHEA. Good.

CHRISTINE *(nods, starts to leave)*. I'll make some coffee.

ALTHEA. You didn't steal your Papa from me, I don't want you thinking that. *(CHRISTINE stops, doesn't look at ALTHEA.)* I know you, you'll get all filled with guilt about it and it's not true.

CHRISTINE *(still not looking at her, nods)*. I'm sorry I said that.

ALTHEA. It wasn't you, it was me. A woman can take it better when she realizes she's just an everyday woman, in an everyday life. It's somehow less of a surprise than for a man. He was a dreamer and I made fun of that. He wanted to sing and play music and make people laugh and dance, and I needed him to keep a job and fix the car. It's no wonder he turned to you, in your eyes he was a hero. He needed that in his everyday life.

CHRISTINE. I was fired three weeks ago.

ALTHEA *(stares at CHRISTINE, dumbfounded)*. What am I going to do with you? *(CHRISTINE shrugs, embarrassed.)* What have you been doing every day when you leave here?

CHRISTINE. Driving, walking, reading.

ALTHEA. Solitude Road.

CHRISTINE. Yeah.

ALTHEA *(kinder than usual)*. Maybe you can show it to me sometime.

CHRISTINE. I know I'm ridiculous, I know you think I'm ridiculous.

ALTHEA *(quietly)*. I don't.

CHRISTINE *(standing apart from ALTHEA, not touching through this scene)*. My first memory is of your hands. The most delicate, the tiniest. I love your hands.

ALTHEA *(looking at her rough, dirty hands)*. Delicate?

CHRISTINE. Holding bits of ribbon and thread, dropping them, one palm to the other. Satiny blue, wispy. I never want to lose...your hands. *(Whispered.)* I don't know how to take the next step.

ALTHEA. Shhh.

CHRISTINE. I wish I was more like you.

ALTHEA. No, you don't.

CHRISTINE. I need you, Mom.

ALTHEA *(turns from CHRISTINE; unsentimental)*. You have what you need, Christine, you always have.

(CHRISTINE watches her mother's back for a moment, makes a decision. She addresses her students. XAVIER appears.)

CHRISTINE. Tit for tat.

XAVIER. Umm?

CHRISTINE. Cooperate on your first move, and then re-
peat whatever move the other player makes. If he coop-
erates, you cooperate; if he aggresses, you aggress. The
most effective survival tactic in all of nature ... Tit for
tat. *(To XAVIER.)* You took my foot, give it back.

XAVIER. You gave it away.

CHRISTINE. I want it back.

XAVIER. No.

CHRISTINE. "No"?

XAVIER. No.

CHRISTINE. I can't need you like this anymore. I need my
foot.

XAVIER. It was your choice to give it away. It can't be
undone.

CHRISTINE. Give me yours. *(He kneels and puts a man's
short, brown boot on her left foot. He still wears her
shoe. She remembers a line from her lecture; thought-
ful.)* "Cooperate with cooperation, confront aggression.
Remember, forgive, trust and be trusted."

XAVIER. *Bien.*

CHRISTINE *(disturbed)*. Are you leaving? Will you ... ?
(He doesn't answer.) I won't know who I am without
you.

XAVIER *(finishes tying the bootstrap, holds her foot in his
hands, kisses it)*. You'll never be without me. *(She
touches his face.)* Close your eyes. *(She does.)* Feel it?

CHRISTINE *(experiences a rush, a shudder)*. I'm tingling.
(She doesn't notice XAVIER leaving.)

XAVIER. Put your head on my chest, I am your father.
Fold me into your arms, I am your child. Twist yourself

around a lover, I am the snake that makes you arch.
When you come, I am the water spilling down your
thigh. I am the water. *(He's gone.)*
CHRISTINE *(quietly)*. Alive. Every cell.

*(JERRY walks in, carrying a bouquet of wildflowers and
a bottle of wine. He sees her and is mystified.)*

CHRISTINE *(laughing a little)*. Medial forebrain bundle ...
JERRY. Hey ... kooky. *(She opens her eyes, unmoving.)*
     Four brains in a bundle? Is that like Three Coins in a
     Fountain? *(No answer.)* What're you doing?
CHRISTINE. I don't know.
JERRY. What's up with your mother? She's gone native.
CHRISTINE. She's digging.
JERRY. I thought I'd come and help you cook.
CHRISTINE. I'm not cooking. Today's not a normal day,
     and I'm not going to pretend it is.
JERRY. What's the matter?
CHRISTINE. I lost my job.
JERRY. Oh, babe, I'm sorry, that's terrible.
CHRISTINE. No. It's okay. I don't know why, but it's
     okay. You have my car keys?
JERRY. Yeah. *(He gets them out of his pocket and gives
     them to her.)* Here you go.
CHRISTINE *(holds on to his hands for a second, then lets
     go)*. I think you'd better get your own car back.
JERRY. Okay.
CHRISTINE. Okay.
JERRY *(searches her face; she is glowing but distant, in-
     scrutable)*. You breaking up with me?
CHRISTINE. Yeah.

JERRY. How'd you know?

CHRISTINE. What?

JERRY. About last night.

CHRISTINE *(realizing what he means)*. Oh. God. I didn't.

JERRY. Jesus.

CHRISTINE. You slept with the girl, Amy?

JERRY. If you didn't know, why are you breaking up with me?

CHRISTINE. I don't want a half-assed life.

JERRY. Ow. Okay, I fucked up. I am in the wrong. I admit it. But you can be civil. I love you. Doesn't that count for anything?

CHRISTINE. Were you loving me the entire time you were fucking her, or, how does that work?

JERRY. Look. I'm sorry.

CHRISTINE. Last night when you lied and smiled and kissed up and walked all over me, were you sorry then? To humiliate me? And me, FUCK ME, I just laid down and took it.

JERRY. I said I'm sorry, I'm sorry. It was a big mistake, I felt bad about it all night.

CHRISTINE. After. You felt bad after.

JERRY. I've been a failure since I got out of college. Everything I touch turns to shit. And now this thing, this little business, is working out, I'm making money, it's doing good, it feels good. This girl, Amy, I was engaged to this girl in college... and then right before we graduated, it was like she knew, like she could smell it on me... and she dumped me. She dumped me and never looked back. She went to law school and married some honcho in Tennessee. Now she's getting a divorce and she called me. It's nothing, nothing's going to come of it.

CHRISTINE. But you wish it would.

JERRY. No. I just wanted to show off. I just wanted her to know I was, you know, not dogshit. *(Beat.)* It was an accident.

CHRISTINE. What, did she trip and fall on your penis?

JERRY. Don't be like this.

CHRISTINE. Be sweet? Be a sport?

JERRY. Come on.

CHRISTINE. Jerry, you know what, I understand. I understand the whole thing, bleeding fucking humanity screws up again. I feel for you. *(Beat.)* But, I'm standing here, too. Not invisible, not a ghost.

JERRY. Okay.

CHRISTINE. We're afraid we're never going to find anyone better. If you could have this other woman, you'd grab her in a second.

JERRY *(after a beat).* You're just depressed about your job.

CHRISTINE. What does that mean, "just depressed." It's a clue. I'm fired, that's a clue. Something's wrong. I don't want to see you anymore. I don't want to see myself anymore.

JERRY *(puts the flowers down on a step, ready to leave).* What are you going to do?

CHRISTINE. I have no idea. I guess I'll have to pay attention for a change.

JERRY *(nodding slowly).* Take it easy. *(He exits through the backyard, addresses ALTHEA.)* Happy hunting, Geronimo.

ALTHEA *(digs two holes, side by side).* I like this body. *(She sits, plants her feet in the holes, buries them with dirt.)* Good body. Good legs. *(She rubs the dirt covering her feet.)* Good hands. So good at doing things. Me, my hands. *(She stands, feet buried, hands up in fists, strong, grasping; fierce.)* J'ai envie ma vie.

(CHRISTINE walks out to the backyard.)

CHRISTINE *(concerned)*. Ma?

(Without looking up, ALTHEA stops CHRISTINE from coming any closer.)

ALTHEA *(to herself)*. J'ai envie ma vie.

CHRISTINE. What's that mean?

ALTHEA *(not looking at CHRISTINE)*. I desire my life.

CHRISTINE. Oh, Ma. I know. We'll get you back on the medicine, we'll...

ALTHEA. No. *(Fists tight.)* There's no hope.

CHRISTINE. There is, we can...

ALTHEA. No. Let me say it... there's no hope. *(She looks at her fists.)* And I don't know what to do when there's no hope. *(Wry.)* It's un-American. All I know how to do is fight.

CHRISTINE. Sometimes standing still is the right move. *(Distant sound of Joe's fiddle.)* "Leave room for grace." Remember that? He used to say "Leave room for grace... " and then he'd play that song... what was... ?

ALTHEA *(with recognition)*. Lache La Patate...

CHRISTINE. Let go the potato?

ALTHEA. Yeah. *(Laughing a little at the absurdity.)* Lache La Patate. What a funny man. Your papa always was a joker. *(To Joe.)* All right. Lache La Patate. *(She rubs her hands together.)*

CHRISTINE. Isn't it, *"Lache PAS La Patate"*? Don't let go, don't give up?

ALTHEA *(finally looks at CHRISTINE; almost playful).* Let go ... don't let go ... let go ... don't let go ... *(She scoops up some of the earth, holds it in her fists. As she speaks she opens her hands and lets the dirt fall.)* Lache. *[Let go.]*

(CHRISTINE catches some of the dirt as it cascades down. A peaceful breath between them, then ...)

CHRISTINE. Can I dig you out?

ALTHEA. For the moment. *(CHRISTINE unearths AL-THEA's feet. ALTHEA unbuttons her nightgown.)* Aren't they strange looking?

CHRISTINE. Hieroglyphics. *(ALTHEA runs her fingers along the lines.)* A secret language.

ALTHEA. What does it say?

CHRISTINE. Tell me.

ALTHEA. It says ... Me. Althea Pitre. I'm still here.

CHRISTINE. I see you, Mom. I see you. *(Beat.)* You see me?

ALTHEA. Mmm.

(ALTHEA sees CHRISTINE, puts her palm on CHRISTINE's cheek. Wearing pajamas, DENISE stands in her bed and addresses the audience.)

DENISE. Sometimes I just feel good for no reason. Like on a day when, because of everything that's going on, I should feel bad, like today, but I don't. I just feel fine, like everything's perfect, even though it doesn't look like it. I mean, I'm punished till college, probably. Chris' mother will think I'm a slut. We'll all be majorly embarrassed. My mother will talk about this, way too much. My grandmother will want to hit me with a belt. And I don't care. I just feel, like, happy. Weird. *(She slashes at the air.)* Sometimes I'm so macho. When I feel this good, I want to be in a fight, against a horrible bad guy and beat the piss out of him. Ta-da. *(She walks around the bed like Miss America.)* Brilliant, beautiful woman, takes no shit, kind to animals. Ladies and gentlemen... *(She strikes a very dramatic pose.)* ...Denise... *(She takes many bows in a very hip way, then proceeds to march down the stairs.)* Make way. Make way. *(She's waving to the crowds, very strong, very proud, very silly.)* Make way for Denise. *(She performs the Miss America wave.)* Elbow, palm, elbow, palm, press the cheek, touch the lace, dry the tear. *(She slashes the air.)* Slay the dragon.

(She parades into the back yard, waving at CHRISTINE and ALTHEA.)

DENISE. Elbow, palm, elbow, palm...

CHRISTINE. What are you doing?.

DENISE. The Miss America Wave. I'm practicing for my future. I'm going to fake them out... *(She delicately mimes a tiny, sweet kiss.)* Kiss the prince... *(She slashes at the air.)* Kill the dragon. *(She glides to ALTHEA with silly pomp and circumstance, kissing and slaying.)* Oh, Deep Blue Grandmother, why are you kneeling in the dirt? You must dance. Dance with Denise of the Future. *(DENISE pulls ALTHEA up.)*

ALTHEA *(feisty)*. Can I put a chastity belt on you?

(Embarrassed, DENISE puts a finger on ALTHEA's mouth to shush her. DENISE slowly spins ALTHEA, as ALTHEA holds her open hands in the air. We hear the faint sounds of a fiddle. The lights begin to fade, lingering on CHRISTINE, watching her mother and her daughter dancing in the garden, a perfect, fleeting moment.)

CHRISTINE. Only for a little while.

(The lights fade.)

END OF PLAY